INTRODUCTION

If introductions bore you, and you'd rather discover what Judge Dredd's face looks like, then turn to page sixty-five now! turn to page sixty-five now! To those readers remaining, welcome to *Judge Dredd Nine*, featuring *2000 AD's* grim guardian of the law and his never-ending task of preventing Mega-City One from sliding into anarchy. Written by John Wagner and Alan Grant, the two adventures in this album reflect the disparate ways in which Dredd maintains civil order in the 22nd Century.

In the seven-part *Cry of the Werewolf* (Progs 322-328) he goes underground to neutralise the source of a radioactive chemical which has spawned a race of werewolves. In *The Wreckers* (Progs 374-375) he leads a squad of judges on the more mundane mission to clean up a gang of Megaway muggers. Both threats, however, are treated with equal seriousness. In the 22nd Century, nothing can be allowed to disturb the peace – be it werewolves or wreckers.

The artwork for the two stories is by Steve Dillon, whose first Dredd in *2000 AD* was *Alone In A Crowd* (Prog 205). "I enjoy drawing Alan Grant and John Wagner's scripts," he told me. "Some writers' picture descriptions are so precise they leave the artist no room to manoeuvre. John and Alan's scripts allow you space to create." *Cry of the Werewolf* attracted Dillon for another reason. "It was over fifty pages long and I knew there would be a chance to develop the secondary characters as the story unfolded."

In the story, Wagner and Grant revitalise the old idea of lycanthropy by giving it a scientific explanation and the Mega-City One treatment. No silver bullets here – just high explosive!

Before drawing the scripts, Dillon watched *The Howling* and *An American Werewolf in London*. Despite the latter being the better werewolf film, he found *The Howling* more useful. The scripts called for some of the victims to remain partially clothed, and thus still recognisably human in form. Dillon compromised by drawing the heads as wolfish as possible while leaving the bodies more or less unchanged.

Research for the scenes set in the undercity was easier. Dillon had spent two weeks in New York and some of the action was set near the hotel he stayed in! "My memory of the area was good," he recalls, "and I drew places like Times Square without any trouble."

Commissioning an artist to draw a seven-part

Above: *A frenzied werewolf!*

Judge Dredd requires careful planning. Four episodes have to be completed before the story can be scheduled. In the four weeks that those episodes are being sent to the printer, the artist produces two more episodes (one every fortnight). In the two weeks that those episodes are running, he produces the seventh and final episode.

Neat as it looks on paper, this method is by no means foolproof. It only needs a bout of flu or some other delay for the artist to be set back. To recover the lost time, he then has to draw quicker than he would like. Towards the end of the serial, Dillon found himself in this situation. However, he managed to complete all seven episodes and still create several memorable scenes.

By the final episode of the story, Dillon was drawing werewolves in his dreams. *The Wreckers* therefore came as a pleasant change. As Dredd embarks on a blitz of sector 27's Megaway muggers, Dillon demonstrates just how well he handles sustained action sequences. Add this to Dillon's view of Mega-City One beset by bad weather and *The Wreckers* stands up well as a raw look at the wilder side of life in the future city.

Judge Dredd defeats the wreckers in just forty-eight hours. But he knows it won't be long before they are back on the streets. While werewolves are easy to defeat once you know how, the problems caused by urban decay can never change.

Steve MacManus, 2000 AD Editor
February 1986

JOHN WAGNER began working in comics at the age of 21. After editorial training (along with Pat Mills) at DC Thomson in Dundee, he became a freelance writer. He has contributed to every major British comic of the 1970s, including Battle *and* 2000 AD *and has written the* Judge Dredd *strip since its inception. He continues to develop new characters and write established ones for* 2000 AD, Battle, Eagle *and other titles.*

ALAN GRANT cut his journalistic teeth with three years editorial work on titles such as Loving, Love Affair *and* Honey. *He began as Sub-Editor on* 2000 AD *in late 1978, and stayed in the post for over a year. He then became a freelance writer, and has since written many comic strips, mainly in collaboration with John Wagner, including* Strontium Dog *and* Judge Dredd.

STEVE DILLON began drawing comics at the age of 16 for Marvel UK, working on Hulk, Nick Fury, *and back-up stories for* Doctor Who Weekly. *In the years since, he has worked for* 2000 AD *including* Judge Dredd, Mean Arena *and* Future Shock *stories, and for* Warrior, *for which he drew* Laser Eraser *and* Pressbutton. *He is currently drawing for* 2000 AD.

Published by Titan Books Ltd., 58 St. Giles High St., London WC2H 8LH, England. Distributed in the United Kingdom and the United States of America by Titan Distributors Ltd., P.O. Box 250, London E3 4RT, England. *Judge Dredd* is © IPC Magazines Ltd. 1986. Printed in England. ISBN 0 907610 56 0. *First edition April 1986.*

JUDGE DREDD

4

RY OF THE EREWOLF

PART 1

SCRIPT
T B GROVER
ART
STEVE DILLON
LETTERING
T FRAME

ON MEGA-CITY ONE, **JUDGE DREDD** MAKES HIS 300TH ARREST OF THE DAY —

CREEP WAS WALKING AROUND WITH A SAWN-OFF STUMP GUN. PUT HIM DOWN FOR **FOUR**.

INSIDE, MEATHEAD.

CONTROL TO ALL UNITS. YOU ARE REMINDED THERE IS A **FULL MOON** TONIGHT. ALL JUDGES WILL BE REQUIRED ON DUTY.

DREDD HERE. BEEN ON THE STREET THIRTY-SIX HOURS SOLID. BETTER BOOK ME **TEN MINUTES** IN THE **SLEEP MACHINE**.

JUSTICE DEPARTMENT'S **T.R.I.'S — TOTAL RELAXATION INDUCERS —** ALLOW A FULL NIGHT'S REST TO BE COMPRESSED INTO TEN MINUTES...

...LEAVING A JUDGE FULLY REFRESHED AND FIT FOR THE MOST ARDUOUS DUTY...

...AND THIS NIGHT **WILL** BE ARDUOUS –

ONE THING ABOUT THIS CITY THAT NEVER CHANGES – FULL MOON ALWAYS BRINGS OUT THE **CRAZIES**.

. . .

TONIGHT, THE MOON WILL BRING OUT **MORE** THAN JUST THE CRAZIES . . .

A CRACK HAS OPENED IN THE FOUNDATIONS OF **NORMAN PITLIK** CITYBLOCK –

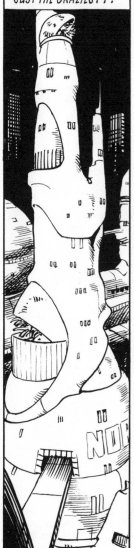

–A CRACK THAT STRETCHES DOWN TO THE **NIGHTMARE WORLD** OF THE **UNDERCITY** !

TONIGHT...THE **WEREWOLF** STALKS !

ARRROOOOOOOOOO

WH-WHAT WAS THAT ?

IT IS TWENTY MINUTES BEFORE JUDGES ARE CALLED TO THE LONELY PEDWAY —

I WAS J-JUST TAKIN' MY EVENING CONSTITUTIONAL WHEN I-I S-SAW 'EM!

CALM DOWN, CITIZEN, IF YOU'RE INNOCENT, YOU'VE NOTHING TO WORRY ABOUT!

IT-IT WASN'T ME, JUDGE! H-H-H-HONEST!

WHAT DO YOU MAKE OF IT, DREDD?

WE CAN RULE *HIM* OUT, ANYWAY. VICTIMS HAVE BEEN RIPPED TO SHREDS AND PARTIALLY *EATEN*. SOME KIND OF *ANIMAL* IS MY GUESS.

ANIMAL? IN *THIS* CITY?

EITHER THAT, OR WE GOT A CITIZEN WHO DOESN'T CUT HIS TOENAILS.

MUNK, PUT OUT A *GENERAL WARNING* AND WAIT HERE TILL FORENSIC ARRIVE.

KORKORAN — WITH ME.

MEANWHILE, ON A A QUIET CITY LINKWAY —

LOOK *OUT*, DARLENE!

OH NO! I'VE *HIT HIM*!

THUDD!

HE'S STILL ALIVE!

WAIT, DARLENE! THERE WAS SOMETHING KINDA FUNNY ABOUT THAT GUY —

JUDGE DREDD

CRY OF THE WEREWOLF

PART 2

A FULL MOON SHINES ON MEGA-CITY ONE — AND SINISTER BEASTS ARE AT LARGE!

THREE DIRECT HITS AND IT'S STILL CLIMBING!

SCRIPT T B GROVER
ART STEVE DILLO
LETTERING T FRAME

I'LL RUN THIS CARCASS DOWN TO **FORENSIC** FOR EXAMINATION. YOU GET THAT WOUND TREATED — NO TELLING **WHAT** YOU MIGHT HAVE PICKED UP FROM THOSE FANGS.

DREDD TO CONTROL — TWO MORE OF THOSE WOLFMEN FOUND. PUT OUT A GENERAL WARNING — COULD BE MORE ABOUT.

AND SEND A SQUAD TO CLEARWAY 433 — THERE'S A BIT OF **CLEANING UP** TO DO.

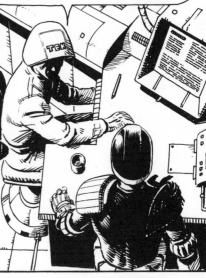

SOON, AT **FORENSIC** — THERE'S THE DATA ON **BRAM.** A GOOD JUDGE, BUT SOME OF HIS DECISIONS WERE BECOMING A BIT **ERRATIC.** HE TOOK THE **LONG WALK** DOWN TO THE **UNDERCITY.**

WHEN A JUDGE'S USEFUL LIFE WAS OVER, HE COULD CHOOSE TO TAKE **THE LONG WALK** — TO BRING **LAW** TO ONE OF THE LAWLESS AREAS BEYOND THE CITY'S BOUNDARIES —

UNDERCITY GATE 31

OPEN THE UNDERCITY GATE!

ONE SUCH AREA WAS THE **UNDERCITY** — THE SEALED-OFF REMAINS OF THE OLD CITY ON WHICH MEGA-CITY ONE HAD BEEN BUILT —

CLANGG!

FAREWELL, BRAM! YOU WILL BE REMEMBERED!

YOU RECKON THIS WEREWOLF **KILLED** BRAM — TOOK HIS UNIFORM.

FROM WHAT I'VE SEEN, THEY'RE NOT EXACTLY **FASHION-CONSCIOUS.**

ACCORDING TO THE RECORDS, BRAM TOOK A BAD *LAS BURN* ON HIS LEFT THIGH BACK IN '99.

MY DOK, DREDD – A LASER SCAR!

DON'T ASK ME HOW, BUT THIS THING IS – OR WAS – **JUDGE BRAM.**

ATTENTION JUDGE DREDD! REPORT TO MED-BAY IMMEDIATELY!

IT'S KORKORAN. SOMETHING'S **HAPPENING** TO HIM –

HE STARTED SPROUTING HAIR A FEW MINUTES AGO. SHAPE OF HIS FACE IS DISTORTING – TEETH ENLARGING – FOAMING AT THE MOUTH...

DROKK! HE'S TURNING INTO A WOLFMAN!

NEXT PROG: **HOWLING FURY!**

RRRR

RRRRRRRR!

"YOU ARE WHAT YOU EAT", THEY SAY... MAYBE THEY SHOULD'VE MADE IT "**YOU ARE WHAT EATS YOU**"!

AND I THOUGHT ALL THAT WEREWOLF BALONEY WAS JUST SUPERSTITION.

OBVIOUSLY NOT. LOCK KORKORAN UP TIGHT. DO WHAT YOU CAN FOR THE OTHERS.

WHERE ARE YOU GOING?

I JUST REMEMBERED — **THE WEREWOLVES HAD ANOTHER VICTIM!**

DREDD RADIOED JUSTICE CENTRAL, AND —

VICTIM'S NAME: DARLENE O'SMITH. RESIDENT APARTMENT 6494M, BUCK CHEGWIN BLOCK.

PUT OUT A PRIORITY ONE — ALL UNITS IN THAT VICINITY TO CONVERGE ON BUCK CHEGWIN!

WITHIN SECONDS, JUDGES ARE RACING UP TO THE CHEGWIN BLOCK —

AROOOOOOOoooo

BUCK CHEGWIN

AROoooo Thap! Thap!

MEANWHILE —

STOP THAT TERRIBLE RACKET!

I'M SURE THEY'VE GOT A DOG IN THERE!

WHAT'S A DOG?

DID YOU HEAR? STOP THAT RACKET OR...I'M...*sending*...for the...judges...

SLAMM!

H-HOLY ANNA! WAS **THAT** A DOG...?

21

CRASHH! GRAAAAR

WHEN JUDGES ARRIVE—

DROKK! WE'RE TOO LATE!

NOW COME ON, DARLENE— WE DON'T WANT TO HURT YOU...

DON'T THINK SHE'S GOT THE MESSAGE!

BADAMM!

BADAM!

DREDD ARRIVES — GET A FLEET OF MEAT WAGONS TO BUCK CHEGWIN!

YOU MISSED ALL THE ACTION, DREDD.

THERE SHE IS — THE LAST OF THE WEREWOLVES!

YOU GOTTA BE JOKING!

I WANT ALL THESE VICTIMS LOCKED UP AND UNDER GUARD. IF THINGS RUN TRUE TO FORM, WE'VE GOT THE MAKINGS OF A **WHOLE WOLFPACK** HERE.

NEXT PROG:

INTO THE NIGHTMARE!

CRY OF THE WEREWOLF

PART 4

SCRIPT
T B GROVER

ART
STEVE DILLON

LETTERING
T FRAME

WEREWOLVES HAVE APPEARED IN MEGA-CITY ONE. NOW, IN THE FORTIFIED **HOLDING PENS** BENEATH THE GRAND HALL OF JUSTICE, THE UNFORTUNATE **VICTIMS** HAVE BEEN ROUNDED UP —

THE CONDITION IS KNOWN AS **LYCANTHROPY** — THE ABILITY TO CHANGE INTO **WOLF FORM**. VICTIMS BECOME FRENZIED **CARNIVORES**, POSSESSED OF **IMMENSE STRENGTH**.

SCANT COMFORT TO **KORKORAN** AND THE OTHERS. ANY PROGRESS ON A **CURE**?

NOT YET, BUT THE LABS HAVE ISOLATED THE **CAUSE** IN THIS CASE.

IN THE TEK LABS— WE FOUND A NEW **RADIOACTIVE CHEMICAL** IN THE BODIES OF THE WEREWOLVES—A SUBSTANCE CAPABLE OF BRINGING ABOUT DRAMATIC CHANGES IN BODY CHEMISTRY. IT'S IDENTIFIABLE BY THE BRIGHT GREENISH GLOW. I CALL IT **CASSIDIUM.**

FAME AT LAST, HUH, CASSIDY?

AW, C'MON—I HAD TO CALL IT SOMETHING.

ANYWAY, I'VE DEVELOPED A **NEUTRALISING AGENT.** WHEN EVEN A **MINUTE** QUANTITY IS ADDED TO THE CASSIDIUM, IT CHANGES IT TO A HARMLESS **ALGAE.**

SO ALL WE'VE GOT TO DO IS **LOCATE** THE **CASSIDIUM** SOURCE.

THERE WE HAVE A HEADSTART, DREDD — **JUDGE BRAM.**

BRAM TOOK THE **LONG WALK** TO THE **UNDERCITY.** IT'S PROBABLE HE PICKED UP THE CONTAMINANT THERE.

THAT'S POSSIBLE. NO TELLING WHAT'S BEEN HAPPENING IN THAT HELLHOLE SINCE THE **APOCALYPSE WAR.**

I WANT **YOU** TO HANDLE THIS, DREDD. FIND THAT SOURCE AND NEUTRALISE IT.

WHAT ABOUT THE WEREWOLVES THEMSELVES? IF THIS CONDITION CAN BE PASSED ON THROUGH THEIR **SALIVA,** THEY'LL HAVE TO BE **ELIMINATED** TOO.

EXACTLY. HAVE FUN.

THANKS.

LATER THAT MORNING —

OPEN THE UNDERCITY GATE !

ROSEMAN TO DREDD !

GLAD I CAUGHT YOU. THOUGHT YOU MIGHT BE INTERESTED...

WE'VE FOUND A **CRACK** IN THE FOUNDATIONS OF **NORMAN PITLIK BLOCK** — RUNS RIGHT DOWN TO THE **UNDERCITY.** PROBABLY HOW THE WEREWOLVES GOT HERE.

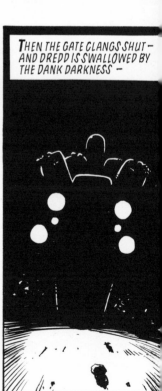

THEN THE GATE CLANGS SHUT — AND DREDD IS SWALLOWED BY THE DANK DARKNESS —

THE UNDERCITY! THE OLD CITY THAT LAY BENEATH THE STREETS OF THE SPRAWLING MEGALOPOLIS.

LONG AGO, IT HAD BECOME SO POLLUTED, SO RUN-DOWN, SO DECAYED THAT JUDGES HAD DECIDED TO CONCRETE OVER IT AND START AGAIN.

NOW IT WAS A REFUGE FOR HALF-HUMANS, MUTANTS, ESCAPED CRIMINALS AND OTHER OUTCASTS FROM THE CITY ABOVE.

PLACE IS SO VAST I COULD SEARCH FOR WEEKS AND GET NOWHERE. BETTER MAKE FOR PITLIK — BOUND TO BE SOME WEREWOLF TRACES THERE.

FOODEE!

FOODEE!

GIVEE FOODEE!

BLIND BEGGARS — BEEN SO LONG IN THE PIT, THEY'VE LOST THE USE OF THEIR EYES.

CLEAR THE WAY!

NO! NO! FIRST GIVEE FOODEE — OR WE TAKEE!

CREEPS WON'T TAKE A TELLING!

BLAM!

CLEAR THE WAY, I SAID!

AIEEE!

27

DREDD FOLLOWS THE TRAIL TO OLD **TIMES SQUARE** —

SONY

ENJOY Coca-Cola

ROCKY 37 ☆ 2 MAD MAX 25 ☆

SIRLOIN STEAK
STEAK & BREW

TRACKS PETER OUT ON THIS HARD SLAB...

BROADWAY... MIGHT AS WELL BE NO WAY!

• • • •

W46 ST

BROADWAY

ONE WAY

SUDDENLY —

RRRUMMBLE!

ROBOTS! FOUND THEMSELVES AN OLD STEAM ENGINE!

GRAAHH!

DROKK! A **WHITE WEREWOLF!**

NEXT PROG: **ASSAULT ON BROADWAY!**

29

JUDGE DREDD HAS BEEN SENT DOWN TO THE UNDERCITY TO NEUTRALISE THE CASSIDIUM SOURCE – THE RADIOACTIVE CHEMICAL WHICH HAS CREATED A RACE OF WEREWOLVES.

THERE, HE COMES UPON A GROUP OF FUGITIVE ROBOTS–

IN THE NAME OF THE LAW – HALT!

SCRIPT
T B GROVER
ART
STEVE DILLON
LETTERING
T FRAME

GRAAAAAA

WANT THE WHITE REWOLF!

WE SLEW **FIFTY** WEREWOLVES TO CAPTURE THIS – THEIR **LEADER**. HE OUR **TROPHY**! THE SYMBOL OF UR DOMINANCE OF **EAST UNDERCITY**!

GONE, UPSIDER JUDGE – YOU PAY THE PRICE FOR ESPASSING ROBOT RRITORY!

BADAM!

BADAM!

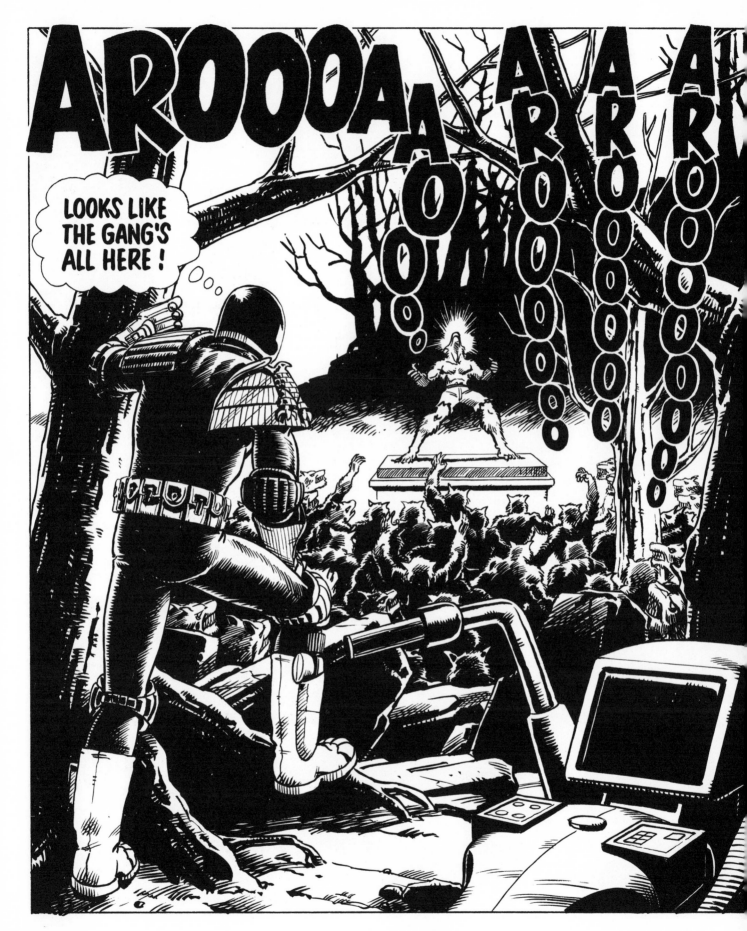

THEN DREDD'S EYE CATCHES SIGHT OF A GHOULISH GREEN GLOW —

CASSIDIUM! A WHOLE LAKE OF THE STUFF!

NO WAY I'M GONNA GET THIS NEUTRALISING AGENT TO THE CASSIDIUM WITHOUT BEING SEEN.

IT'LL HAVE TO BE STRAIGHT THROUGH THEM — AND HOPE FOR THE BEST!

BIKE CANNON!

VRMMM!

BUDDA BUDDA

GRAIEEEE

DOWN, FIDO!

HERE GOES NOTHIN'!

BLAM! BLAM!

THE CONCENTRATED NEUTRALISING AGENT SPREADS THROUGH THE POOL, TURNING THE DEADLY CASSIDIUM INTO A HARMLESS BROWN ALGAE —

I'LL SAY THIS FOR CASSIDY — HIS STUFF WORKS!

BUT WHETHER I'LL EVER GET BACK TO TELL HIM IS ANOTHER MATTER!

GRAAA!

GRAAAH!

NEXT PROG: **ONCE BITTEN, TWICE DOOMED!**

CRY OF THE WEREWOLF

GRAAAAIEI

PART 6

THE UNDERCITY – THE DECAYING RUINS BENEATH MEGA-CITY ONE – WHERE JUDGE DREDD HAS NEUTRALISED THE CHEMICAL POOL WHICH SPAWNED A RACE OF WEREWOLVES.

NOW, DREDD MUST ESCAPE THE BLOOD-CRAZED PACK!

BADAM! BADAM!

BUDDA! BUDDA! BUDDA! BUDDA!

SCRIPT
T B GROVER
ART
STEVE DILLON
LETTERING
T FRAME

ABOVE THE MELEE, THE **WEREWOLF LEADER** ANTICIPATES THE BLOODY RESULT OF THE CONFRONTATION —

BADAM!

—AND MOVES TO FORESTALL THE ESCAPE!

AROOO OO!

WITH FIRE AND FURY, DREDD CLEAVES HIS PATH —

ROLL OVER, ROVER! I'M COMIN' THROUGH!

HIGH EXPLOSIVE!

BADAAAM!

BEHIND DREDD, THE HOWLING PACK PAUSES—DAUNTED...

...AND HAVING CONSIDERED THE **PERIL** OF **PURSUIT**, TURNS BACK TO **GORGE** ON THE REMAINS OF THEIR FALLEN COMPANIONS!

AROOOO

RIPPPP!

I'M THROUGH — BUT MY BUSINESS WITH THE WEREPACK IS FAR FROM OVER.

THE SOURCE IS DESTROYED — BUT THE CONDITION CAN BE PASSED ON BY THE WEREWOLVES' BITE.

BEFORE THE CITY ABOVE CAN BE SAFE, EVERY LAST WEREWOLF MUST DIE!

GRRAAAHHHH!

THE WHITE WEREWOLF!

NAAAAR!

BEING CUT TO RIBBONS! GOTTA REACH MY GUN —

CRY OF THE WEREWOLF

PART 7

SCRIPT
T B GROVER

ART
STEVE DILLON

LETTERING
T FRAME

THE UNDERCITY! ON A CRUMBLING WALKWAY SPANNING A RAD-PIT THE WEREWOLF PACK HAVE BEEN LURED BY THE CRY OF THEIR LEADER.

THERE THEY GATHER IN CONFUSION. THEIR LEADER — THE WHITE WEREWOLF — IS DEAD... AND THE GHASTLY CRY COMES FROM A JUDGE'S LAWMASTER —

AROOOOOOOO

FROM ITS PLACE OF CONCEALMENT A GRISLY **CLAW** CREEPS TOWARDS A **RADIO DETONATOR** —

JUDGE DREDD'S **LAST ACT** AS A HUMAN BEING!

KABOOM! KABOOM!

THE **WEREPACK** PLUNGES TO ITS **DOOM** IN THE DEADLY **RADIATION HEAT** OF THE **RAD-PIT** BELOW!

JUDGE DREDD — OR WHAT WAS **ONCE** JUDGE DREDD — UTTERS A PIERCING **HOWL** OF TRIUMPH!

GRAAAEEEEE!

AR-ROOOOO

THEN HE TURNS FROM THE SEARING HEAT OF THE RAD-PIT... STUMBLES AWAY –

HIS DECISION TO FOLLOW THE WEREWOLVES TO THEIR DOOM IS FORGOTTEN. THE WHITE WEREWOLF'S **BITE MARKS** ARE STILL ETCHED IN HIS FLESH – AND ONLY ONE CRAVING CONSUMES HIM...

BLOODLUST!

IT IS NOT LONG BEFORE HIS KEENING SENSES DETECT THAT DELICIOUS SCENT –

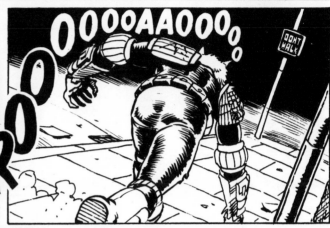

AROOOOOOOOAAOOOOO

DONT WALK

HOLY CRIPES! IT-IT'S ONE O' THEM **WOLFIES!**

KEEP CALM. STICK TO THE PLAN.

RRRRRR

BACK SLOWLY AWAY.

HERE, WOLFIE! HERE, BOY!

BUT AS THE AGING JUDGE'S FINGER TIGHTENS . . .

DROKK! IT'S IN A JUDGE'S UNIFORM . . . AND THAT BADGE — **DREDD!**

CAN THAT **THING** BE **JOE DREDD?**

AND IF SO, WHAT DO I **DO** WITH HIM?

IF IT IS DREDD, 'LEAST HE DESERVES IS A HERO'S DEATH. BETTER TAKE HIM BACK UP TO THE CITY — LET THEM DECIDE.

STUMM GAS!

FWOOMPH!

NAAAARRR

THE CHOKING VAPOUR TAKES INSTANT EFFECT —

DREDD OR NOT, CAN'T RISK YOU WAKING UP AND TAKING A CHUNK OUTA ME.

PRAGER MAKES HIS WAY THROUGH THE UNDERCITY. IT HAS BEEN HIS TERRITORY FOR THE LAST FOUR YEARS. THE INHABITANTS KNOW HIM WELL, AND GIVE HIM GROUND.

AT THE CITY GATE —

CLANG! CLANG!

WHO GOES THERE?

JUDGE PRAGER. TOOK THE LONG WALK FOUR YEARS BACK. GOT SOMETHIN' FOR YOU.

A JUDGE ALL RIGHT. WHAT YOU GOT FOR US, PRAGER?

THIS.

DROKK! DREDD! SO THE WEREWOLVES GOT HIM!

I'D BETTER GET HIM TO MED-BAY, QUICK.

HIS TASK DONE, PRAGER RETURNS TO THE GLOOM BELOW —

HEY, PRAGER — HOW'S THINGS DOWN THERE ANYWAY?

GRIM.

CLANGG!

LATER, IN A HALL OF JUSTICE MED-BAY –

HE'S COMING ROUND!

KORKORAN... YOU'RE...NORMAL AGAIN!

SO ARE **YOU**, DREDD.

YOU'RE RIGHT! BUT HOW – ?

CASSIDY HERE CAME UP WITH THE CURE. GUY'S A GENIUS – ONLY TROUBLE IS, HE NEVER LETS YOU FORGET IT.

WELL, YOU GOT MY THANKS ANYWAY, CASSIDY.

I DON'T MIND ADMITTING, FOR A WHILE DOWN THERE, THINGS GOT **PRETTY HAIRY!**

NEXT PROG: THE WRECKERS!

YOU SEE THE SIGN AS YOU COME OUT OF **SECTOR 26** ON THE THROUGHWAY. SECTOR 27 WAR DAMAGE ZONE AHEAD — **BEWARE OF WRECKERS.**

SECTOR 27 WAR DAMAGE ZONE AHEAD

BEWARE OF WRECKERS

MINIMUM SPEED **250 KPH**

ONE WAY

SOME PEOPLE CHICKEN OUT AT THE LAST MINUTE — TAKE THE DETOUR. BUT NOT YOU . . .

JUSTICE DEPT. RECOMMENDED DETOUR **GET IN LANE**

WHY DO YOU HUNCH DOWN TIGHTER IN YOUR SEAT AS YOU PASS THE LAST NEON WARNINGS?

MAINTAIN SPEED CLOSE ALL WINDOWS DO NOT STOP FOR ANY REASON

'COS THE **WRECKERS** ARE OUT THERE — AND TONIGHT COULD BE **YOUR** NIGHT!

OH NO! AND ADD **50 KILOMETRES** TO YOUR JOURNEY? YOU GOTTA BE JOKING!

YOU'VE MADE THIS RUN PLENTY TIMES BEFORE. NOTHIN' EVER HAPPENED. NOTHIN' WILL HAPPEN TONIGHT.

SO WHY ARE YOU **SWEATING**?

THE WRECKERS!

PART 1

LET'S DO IT!

NO ENTRY

SCRIPT
T B GROVER
ART
STEVE DILLON
LETTERING
T FRAME

54

ONLY ONE WAY TO STOP THIS —

BIKE CANNON!

BUDDA! BUDDA!

AAGH!

JUDGES CONVERGING FROM OTHER DIRECTIONS ROUND UP ONE OR TWO —

URRG!

UNNH!

BUT THE **WRECKERS** ARE MELTING AWAY — DISAPPEARING INTO THE NIGHTMARE LANDSCAPE...

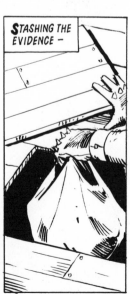

STASHING THE EVIDENCE —

BECOMING ORDINARY CITIZENS AGAIN.

AND IF THE NEIGHBOURS SUSPECT ANYTHING... WHY, THEY WON'T SAY A WORD. THEIR HUSBANDS ARE PROBABLY OUT THERE WRECKING TOO!

TWO WRECKERS DEAD — FOUR CAPTURED. SMALL CHANGE, AS USUAL!

AND NO TIME TO FOLLOW UP ON THE OTHERS.

ATTENTION ALL UNITS VICINITY B. HAYNES WAY. WRECKING IN PROGRESS!

RENSKI, TAKE CARE OF THINGS HERE! THE REST OF YOU — RIDE!

NEXT DAY, DREDD SEES THE CHIEF JUDGE —

THE WRECKERS IN SECTOR 27 ARE GETTING OUT OF HAND. IT'S TIME WE CRACKED DOWN. I WANT YOU IN CHARGE OF THE OPERATION.

I'M PULLING IN 100 JUDGES FROM OTHER DETAILS. THAT'S ALL WE CAN SPARE, I'M AFRAID.

YOU HAVE 48 HOURS. CLEAN OUT THE WRECKERS!

CONSIDER 'EM CLEANED!

NEXT PROG· **CRACK DOWN — CRACK UP!**

57

FROM HIS APARTMENT WINDOW, *JOE GIBBS* PEERS OUT ON THE NIGHTMARE LANDSCAPE OF SECTOR 27.

DARKNESS IS FALLING. A *MIST* IS CREEPING IN OVER THE WAR-TORN TERRAIN.

SECTOR 27

EAST 6

RECKON I'LL GO OUT FOR A WHILE.

A GOOD NIGH

TH

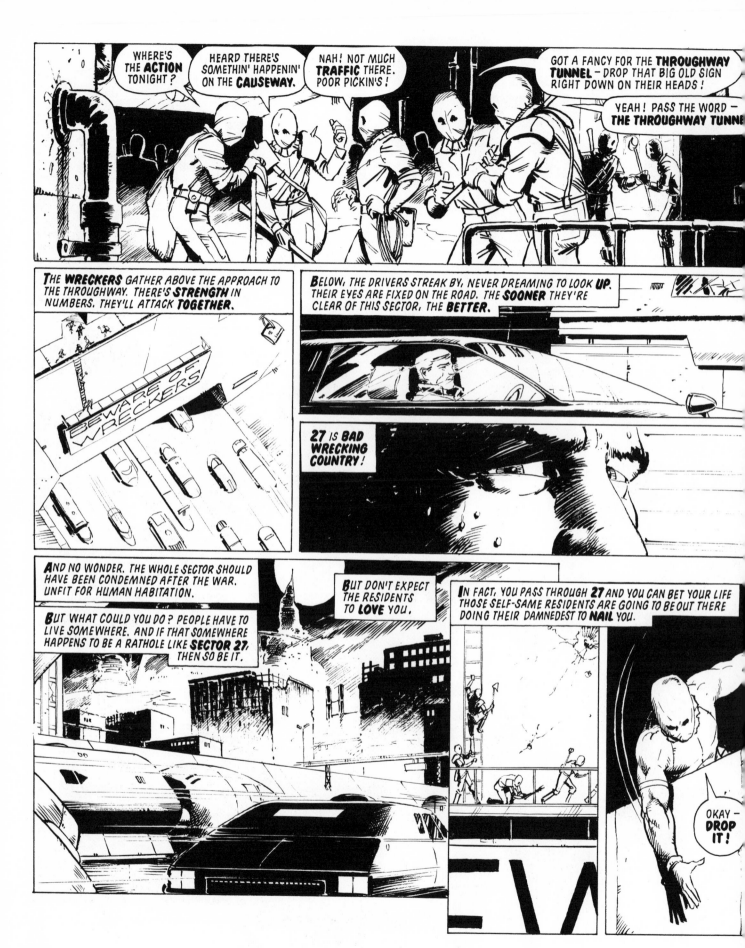

WHERE'S THE **ACTION** TONIGHT?

HEARD THERE'S SOMETHIN' HAPPENIN' ON THE **CAUSEWAY**.

NAH! NOT MUCH **TRAFFIC** THERE. POOR PICKIN'S!

GOT A FANCY FOR THE **THROUGHWAY TUNNEL** — DROP THAT BIG OLD SIGN RIGHT DOWN ON THEIR HEADS!

YEAH! PASS THE WORD — **THE THROUGHWAY TUNNE**

THE **WRECKERS** GATHER ABOVE THE APPROACH TO THE THROUGHWAY. THERE'S **STRENGTH** IN NUMBERS. THEY'LL ATTACK **TOGETHER**.

BEWARE OF WRECKERS

BELOW, THE DRIVERS STREAK BY, NEVER DREAMING TO LOOK **UP**. THEIR EYES ARE FIXED ON THE ROAD. THE **SOONER** THEY'RE CLEAR OF THIS SECTOR, THE **BETTER**.

27 IS BAD WRECKING COUNTRY!

AND NO WONDER. THE WHOLE SECTOR SHOULD HAVE BEEN CONDEMNED AFTER THE WAR. UNFIT FOR HUMAN HABITATION.

BUT WHAT COULD YOU DO? PEOPLE HAVE TO LIVE SOMEWHERE. AND IF THAT SOMEWHERE HAPPENS TO BE A RATHOLE LIKE **SECTOR 27**, THEN SO BE IT.

BUT DON'T EXPECT THE RESIDENTS TO **LOVE** YOU.

IN FACT, YOU PASS THROUGH **27** AND YOU CAN BET YOUR LIFE THOSE SELF-SAME RESIDENTS ARE GOING TO BE OUT THERE DOING THEIR DAMNEDEST TO **NAIL** YOU.

OKAY — **DROP IT!**

THE WRECKERS ARE TRAPPED IN THE TUNNEL —

BUDDA! BUDDA!

AAAH!

JUDGES!

HALF DREDD'S FORCE APPROACH FROM THE SECTOR 26 END —

YOU'RE SURROUNDED, CREEPS! SURRENDER WHILE YOU CAN!

AGHH!!

NOT ONE WRECKER ESCAPES —

26 SIDE SECURE, DREDD!

GOOD WORK! CATCH WAGONS AND MED-SQUADS, MOVE IN!

IT IS FORTUNATE FOR JOE GIBBS THAT HE CHOSE THE **CAUSEWAY** WRECKING —

JUDGES! SCATTER!

HERE THERE ARE MORE **ESCAPE ROUTES** — MORE CHANCES OF **LOSING** YOURSELF AMONG THE RUINS —

STOP — OR I FIRE!

AAAH!

HOLY MOLEY! NEVER SAW SO MANY JUDGES!

HEGLER TO DREDD. WE GOT 14 WRECKERS UNDER WRAPS, ANOTHER 11 FOR THE MEAT WAGON. RECKON ABOUT 10 GOT AWAY.

OKAY — IMMEDIATE HOUSE TO HOUSE SEARCH. I'LL KEEP 40 JUDGES ON RESERVE, SEND THE REST TO YOU.

IT TAKES TWENTY HAIR-RAISING MINUTES FOR JOE GIBBS TO REACH HIS APARTMENT —

JOE! WHAT HAPPENED?

BIG JUDGE **CRACK-DOWN**... I WAS LUCKY TO GET **AWAY.**

CRASH!

63

ROUTINE SEARCH, CITIZEN. NOTHING TO WORRY ABOUT — UNLESS YOU'VE GOT SOMETHING TO **HIDE**.

THESE BLOODSTAINS. **EXPLAIN!**

I...ER...

WE FOUND THIS DISGUISE UNDER THE FLOOR OF THE NEXT DOOR APARTMENT.

IT'S NOT MINE! I'VE NEVER SEEN IT BEFORE!

WE'LL SEE WHAT YOUR STORY IS WHEN FORENSIC HAVE FINISHED WITH YOU. **MOVE!**

YOU TOO, CITIZEN.

THAT NIGHT AND THE NEXT, DREDD'S FORCE KEEPS UP ITS RELENTLESS PRESSURE ON THE WRECKERS. WHEN THE 48 HOURS ALLOTTED TO THE CRACK-DOWN ARE UP, SECTOR 27 IS **QUIET**.

OPERATION COMPLETED. ALL PERSONNEL RETURN TO NORMAL DUTIES.

DREDD KNOWS HE HASN'T **CURED** THE PROBLEM. HE HASN'T CAUGHT **ALL** THE WRECKERS. AND IN ANY CASE, A SEWER LIKE SECTOR 27 **BREEDS** WRECKERS.

AND SOMETIME — AND IT WON'T BE LONG — HE'LL BE ON PATROL AND HE'LL HEAR THE MESSAGE COMING THROUGH —

ATTENTION ALL JUDGES VICINITY 27 STRIPWAY — WRECKING IN PROGRESS!

AND HE'LL KNOW SECTOR 27 IS **BUZZING** AGAIN.

THE END